*Jenny Dyer*

# RODEO DOWNUNDER

First Published 2007 by
Cooloola Colour Graphics
9 Barter Street
Gympie Q 4570
Australia

For further information or to order photographs visit:
*www.cooloola.com*
*www.rodeodownunder.com*

ISBN  978-0-9804193-0-6

Cover and Artwork: Jenny Dyer

Photography: Jenny Dyer

Dedicated to the Loving Memory of my Dad, Tom Hawkins, who was associated with the Widgee Rodeo for over 50 years and also to my husband and brothers who carry on this tradition.

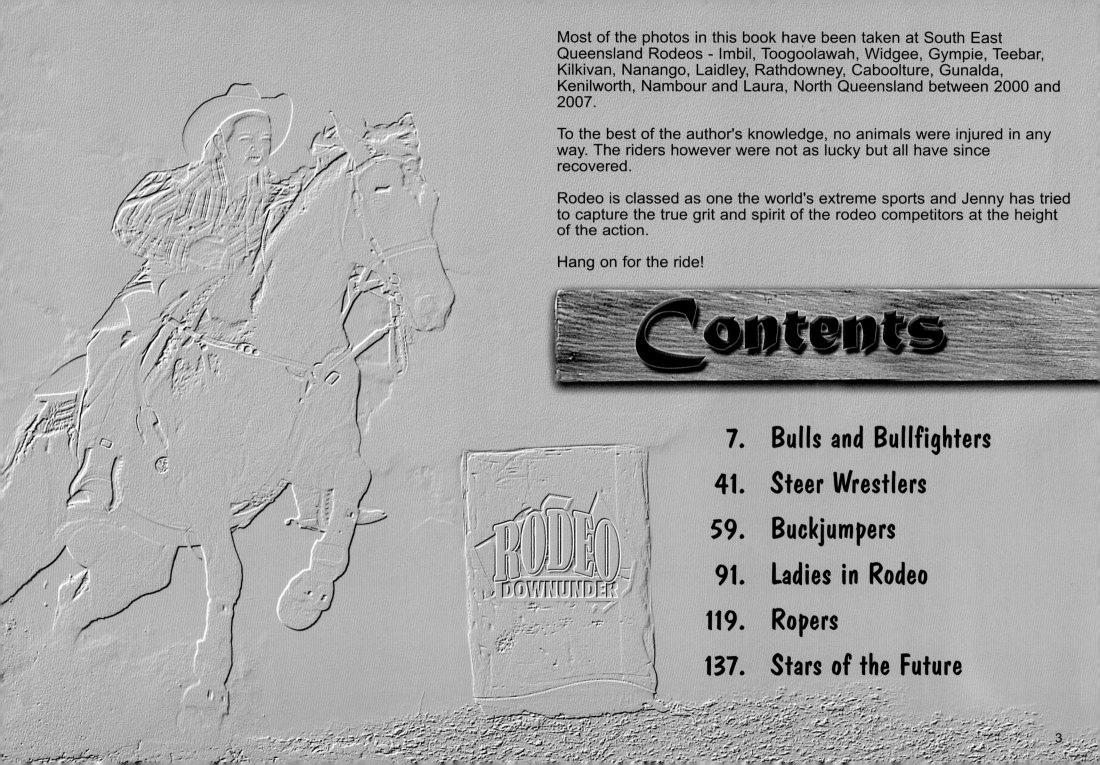

Most of the photos in this book have been taken at South East Queensland Rodeos - Imbil, Toogoolawah, Widgee, Gympie, Teebar, Kilkivan, Nanango, Laidley, Rathdowney, Caboolture, Gunalda, Kenilworth, Nambour and Laura, North Queensland between 2000 and 2007.

To the best of the author's knowledge, no animals were injured in any way. The riders however were not as lucky but all have since recovered.

Rodeo is classed as one the world's extreme sports and Jenny has tried to capture the true grit and spirit of the rodeo competitors at the height of the action.

Hang on for the ride!

# Contents

7.   Bulls and Bullfighters

41.   Steer Wrestlers

59.   Buckjumpers

91.   Ladies in Rodeo

119.   Ropers

137.   Stars of the Future

# Bull Riding

This is the most dangerous rodeo sport and most loved by rodeo fans. The rider has to stay on the bucking mountain of muscle for eight seconds, hanging on with one hand only and not touching down with the other. If they last their time, the judge awards the bull rider a score.

Riders can get hung up (unable to free their hand) if they come off the wrong way. The bullfighters or clowns are there to help the rider out of danger when things turn nasty and often put their own bodies on the line to protect them.

5

You can almost feel the pain!

RODEO DOWNUNDER

PH 071'271128

RODEO
DOWNUNDER

RODEO
DOWNUNDER

RODEO DOWNUNDER

RODEO
DOWNUNDER

Seeing Stars! The bull was later named "Knock Out Barry".

RODEO
DOWNUNDER

RODEO
DOWNUNDER

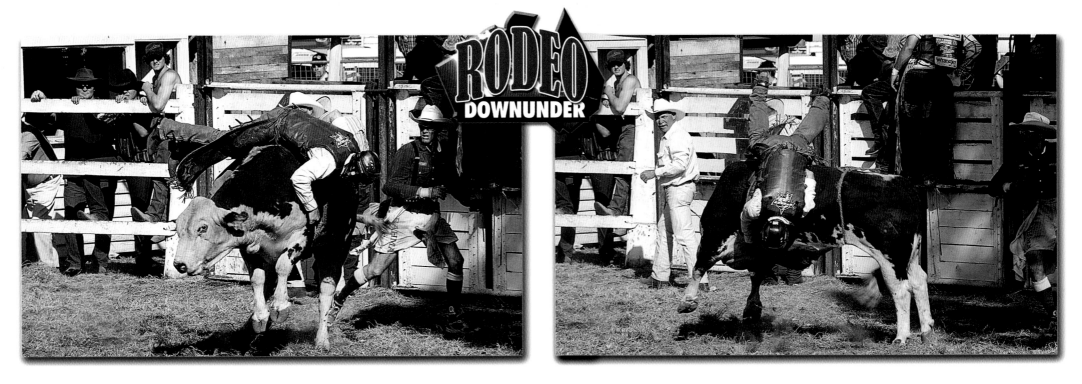

RODEO
DOWNUNDER

23

RODEO
DOWNUNDER

RODEO
DOWNUNDER

RODEO
DOWNUNDER

RODEO
DOWNUNDER

32

RODEO
DOWNUNDER

RODEO
DOWNUNDER

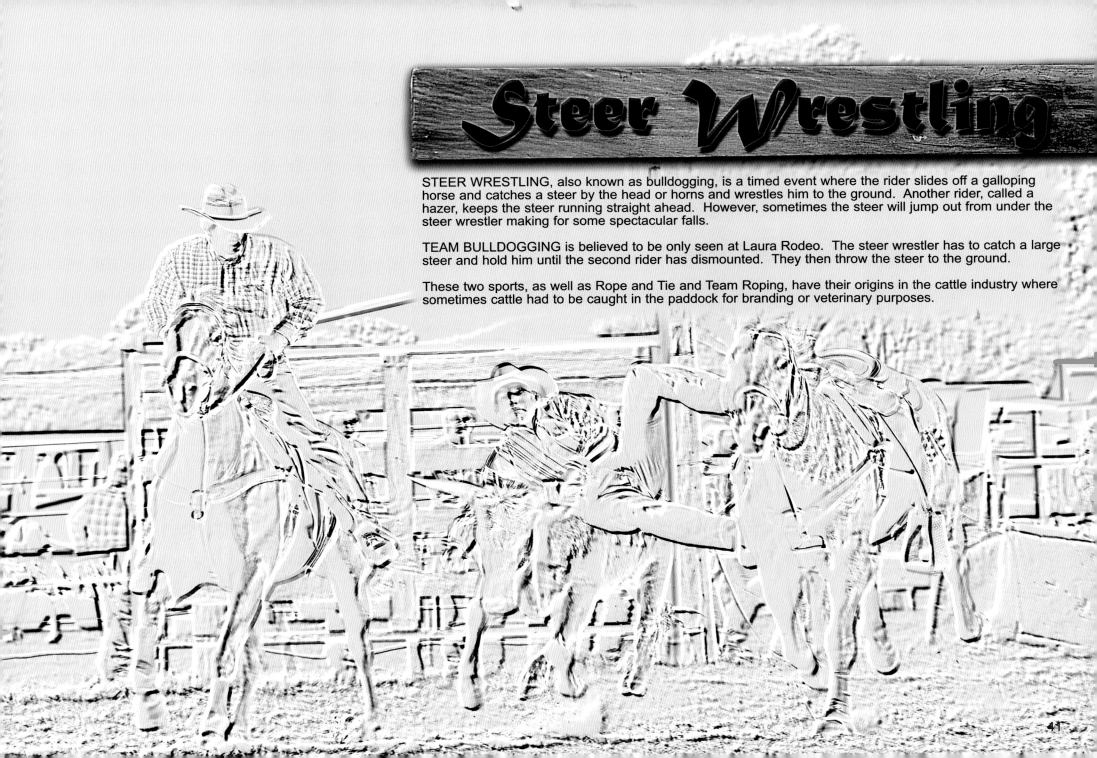

# Steer Wrestling

STEER WRESTLING, also known as bulldogging, is a timed event where the rider slides off a galloping horse and catches a steer by the head or horns and wrestles him to the ground. Another rider, called a hazer, keeps the steer running straight ahead. However, sometimes the steer will jump out from under the steer wrestler making for some spectacular falls.

TEAM BULLDOGGING is believed to be only seen at Laura Rodeo. The steer wrestler has to catch a large steer and hold him until the second rider has dismounted. They then throw the steer to the ground.

These two sports, as well as Rope and Tie and Team Roping, have their origins in the cattle industry where sometimes cattle had to be caught in the paddock for branding or veterinary purposes.

RODEO
DOWNUNDER

RODEO
DOWNUNDER

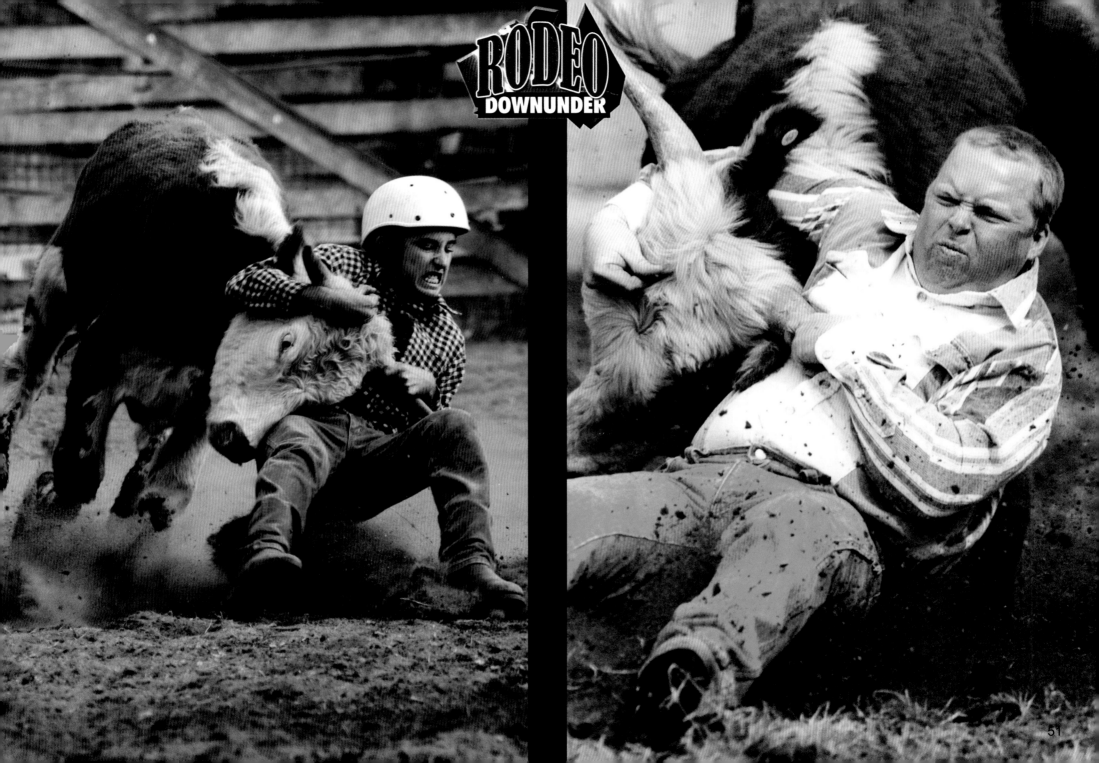

RODEO
DOWNUNDER

# Buckjumpers

The bronc rider must mark out of the shute (heels must be on the horse's shoulder before the horse hits the ground) and then survive eight seconds of bucking fury without touching down. The rider is scored for his ability to endure the twisting, turning, bucking action.

SADDLE BRONC riders use a saddle and one rope rein whereas the BAREBACK RIDER uses special rigging with a handle placed at the horse's withers. They are two very different styles of riding. The bareback rider requires great strength and balance and his muscles and joints endure much strain and stress trying to hold onto the horse.

The pickup men position themselves to help the rider dismount safely.

This sport has its origins in horse breaking the old fashioned way.

59

RODEO
DOWNUNDER

RODEO
DOWNUNDER

RODEO DOWNUNDER

Peter Tapsall
LIVESTOCK & GENERAL TRANSPORT
PH. 41 632 599

63

Getting back on its feet, the horse was okay. The rider broke several ribs.

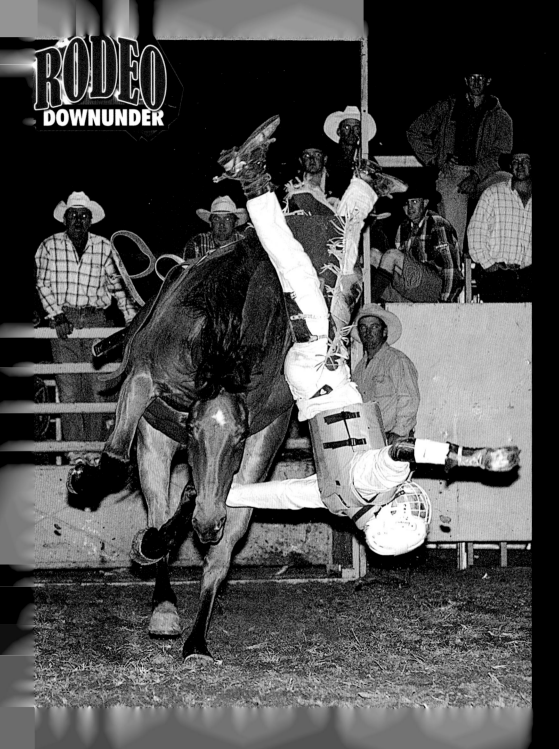

RODEO
DOWNUNDER

This cowboy's escape wasn't so lucky. The horse actually rolled over the top of him. You can see his head in the dust in the bottom photo.

RODEO
DOWNUNDER

71

RODEO
DOWNUNDER

RODEO
DOWNUNDER

73

RODEO
DOWNUNDER

(07) 54836766

WIDGEE Mobile
SANDBLASTING
840 126

STOCK CRATES
HORSE FLOATS
TRUCKS
TRAILERS

A Hint of Class
BEAUTY SALON

COMPLETE HAIR SALON
KERATIN THERAPY
FOILS for ACRYLIC
WAXING
LASH for BROW
TINTING

ACTION FORD

TOM
GRADY

TOM GRADY

BREAKAWAY ROPING is a timed event where the rider ropes a calf. The rope is not secured to the saddle and breaks away leaving the calf to run on. Penalties are incurred for breaking the time box barrier.

The BARREL RACING rider races against the clock around three barrels in a clover leaf pattern. Time penalties are imposed for knocking over the barrels.

STEER UNDECORATING is a timed event where the rider has to chase a steer and detach a ribbon glued on the steer's shoulder. A hazer keeps the steer from veering away from the competitor. This is one of the most dangerous ladies' events, which sometimes results in spectacular falls.  Penalties are incurred for breaking the time box barrier.

Ladies in Rodeo

There are only a few girls gutsy enough to ride bulls. The clowns were quick to help out Shea Fisher when she was hung up. Luckily they were able to lift her off the ground to free her hand quickly.

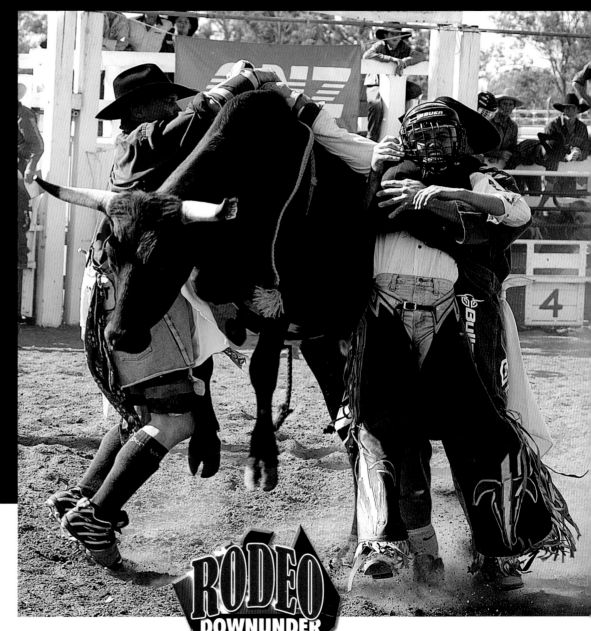

RODEO
DOWNUNDER

RODEO
DOWNUNDER

RODEO DOWNUNDER

117

ROPE AND TIE is a timed event which starts with the rider in the time box.
The horse and rider work as a team to catch, hold and tie the calf. If he breaks the
time box barrier, before the calf is released, there is a time penalty. Arms in the air
at the end of the manoeuvre signals to the flag judge that his calf is secured and he
has finished his run.

TEAM ROPING requires two team members, the header roping the head of the
steer and the heeler roping the back legs in the shortest possible time.
Time penalties are incurred for breaking the barrier and one-legged catches.

Calf Ropers

RODEO
DOWNUNDER

RODEO
DOWNUNDER

COLTS

130

RODEO DOWNUNDER

133

Stars of the Future

RODEO
DOWNUNDER

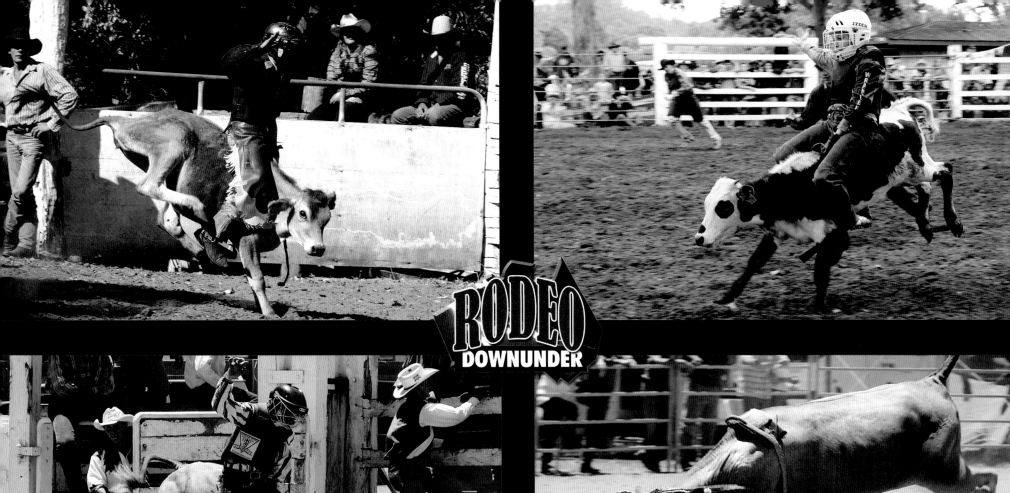

RODEO
DOWNUNDER

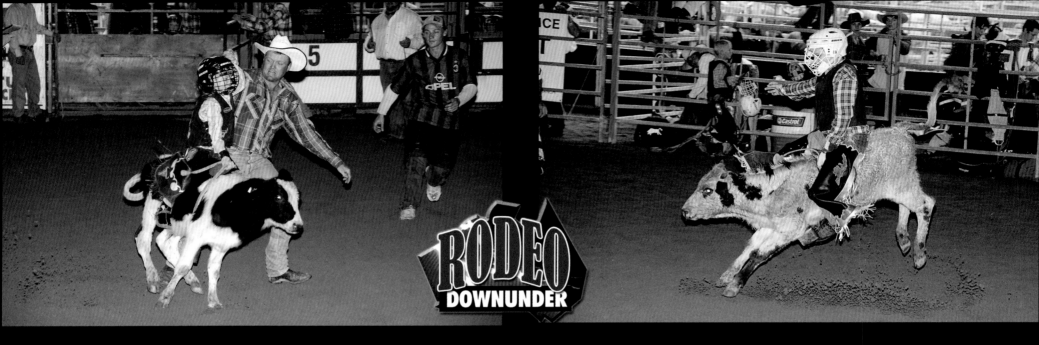

THANKS: To all those competitors for giving me so many photo opportunities; Jocelyn Frahm and the National Rodeo Association for all their help over the years; Emily, Kylie, Erin, Shannon, Gail and Yolanda for their continuous and honest advice and help; Donna Neilson for her time in proofreading; Janine, from Australian Performance Horse Magazine; and a special thank you to Barry, who has patiently helped me carry my camera gear, for his advice, encouragement and help when I have spent all day - daylight to dusk and sometimes midnight photographing.

# INDEX

Although every attempt has been made to ensure accuracy in identifying the riders, some errors may exist. We apologise for any errors.

| Page | Caption |
|---|---|
| 4 | Denae Hart, Christine Balantinacz carrying the flag and John Gordon at the finals at Caboolture Rodeo. |
| 6 | Troy Wolgast with bullfighter Barry McIntyre, Rathdowney Rodeo |
| 8 | Nathan Sherlock, Kilkivan Rodeo |
| 9 | Bullfighter - Dan Keliher and Rory Smith, Imbil Rodeo |
| 10 | Dave Atkinson, Teebar Rodeo |
| 12 | Mick Chapman, Teebar Rodeo |
| 14 | Peter Williamson, Widgee Rodeo |
| 15 | Bullfighter (red shirt) Joe Mooney |
| 16 | Unknown |
| 17 | Barry McIntyre (bullfighter on ground) and Dan Keliher (bullfighter), Widgee Rodeo |
| 18 | Steven Taylor, Ben Keliher (bullfighter), Teebar Rodeo |
| 20 | Malcolm Wieland and Steve Brown, Imbil Rodeo |
| 21 | Bullfighters, Dan Keliher (above) and Dave Kennedy |
| 22 | Shane Egan, Imbil Rodeo |
| 23 | Dan Keliher (bullfighter), Imbil Rodeo |
| 24 | Bullfighter - Dave Kennedy, Imbil Rodeo |
| 25 | Bullfighers - Dave Kennedy & Dan Keliher, Imbil Rodeo |
| 26 | Justin Voll with bullfighters Darren Janke and Barry McIntyre, Imbil Rodeo |
| 28 | Saras Ramsay, Darren Janke (bullfighter) |
| 29 | Bullfighters, Darren Janke and Barry McIntyre |
| 30 | Unknown |
| 31 | Darren Janke - Bullfighter |
| 32 | Reece Weller rider and Stuart Grayson, Widgee Rodeo |
| 33 | Bullfighter, Clinton Clem, Widgee Rodeo |
| 34 | Casey Morris, Widgee. Bullfighter, Clinton Clem |
| 35 | Bullfighters, Clinton Clem & Darren Janke. |
| 36 | Martin Carlo, Widgee Rodeo |
| 37 | Darcy Nixon-Smith, Widgee Rodeo |
| 38 | Klint Lee, Kenilworth Rodeo |
| 40 | Shanae Payne, Widgee Rodeo |
| 42 | Brad Cavanagh and Dean Porter, Teebar Rodeo |
| 43 | Ryan Sainsbury, Teebar Rodeo |
| 44 | Brad Henry and Scott Peters, Teebar Rodeo |
| 45 | Jordan O'Neill and Barry McIntyre with Brad Cavanagh (Hazer), Imbil Rodeo |
| 46 | Ian Allen, Imbil Rodeo |
| 47 | Jim Brokenbrough, Imbil Rodeo, Ben Ruhle, Kenilworth Rodeo, Lachlan O'Neill, Teebar Rodeo |
| 48 | John Gordon and Marcus Jones, Widgee Rodeo |
| 49 | Marcus Jones, Widgee Rodeo |
| 50 | Mark Hogno, Widgee Rodeo |
| 51 | Jordan O'Neill, Widgee Rodeo. Shane Hart, Teebar Rodeo. |
| 52 | Peter Young, Widgee Rodeo |
| 53 | Steve Sutherland and Adam Purse, Toogoolawah Rodeo |
| 54 | Clinton Clem, Gympie Rodeo |
| 55 | Hugh Steggall, Widgee Rodeo |
| 56 | Robert Bunn and Brad Cavanagh, Laura Rodeo |
| 58 | Peta Browne, Caboolture Rodeo |
| 60 | James O'Toole and Dene Barram (Pickup), Kilkivan Rodeo |
| 62 | Dinny Moran, Teebar Rodeo |
| 63 | Greg Meech, Nanango Rodeo |
| 64 | Mark Stevenson (Rider) and Ross Siebenhausen, Teebar Rodeo |
| 66 | Matty Makinson, Gympie Rodeo |
| 67 | Rance Makinson, Kilkivan Rodeo |
| 68 | Michael Hodder and Kerry Hall (Pickup), Teebar Rodeo |
| 69 | Peter Young (Pickup) |
| 70 | Unknown, Rathdowney Rodeo |
| 71 | Unknown, Rathdowney Rodeo |
| 72 | Bernie Hamilton, Imbil Rodeo |
| 74 | Matty Makinson, Widgee Rodeo |
| 75 | BJ Shepherd, Kilkivan Rodeo |
| 76 | Dale Roberts |
| 77 | Greg Meech, Imbil Rodeo |
| 78 | Heath Wallace, Teebar Rodeo |
| 79 | Bill Church, Kenilworth Rodeo |
| 80 | Rance Makinson, Caboolture Rodeo |
| 81 | Stuart Grayson (Pickup), Widgee Rodeo |
| 82 | James O'Toole, Imbil Rodeo |
| 83 | Barry Creevey, Nanango Rodeo |
| 84 | Heath Wallace, Widgee Rodeo |
| 85 | Bill Church and Robbie Hamilton, Widgee Rodeo |
| 86 | Darren Milburn (Pickup) |
| 87 | Heath Wallace on Forest Gump, Imbil Rodeo |
| 88 | Dale Derrick, Widgee Rodeo |
| 89 | Jason Hall, Stuart Grayson (Pickup), Widgee Rodeo |
| 90 | Stacey Freeman, Teebar Rodeo |
| 92 | Shea Fisher, Toogoolawah Rodeo |
| 94 | Tammy Hancock, Kenilworth Rodeo |
| 95 | Judy Gough, Teebar Rodeo |
| 96 | Tamara Knox |
| 97 | Rebecca Leeson, Kenilworth Rodeo |
| 98 | Stephanie Young, Caboolture Rodeo |
| 99 | Casey Clarke, Imbil Rodeo |
| 100 | Camille O'Toole, Widgee Rodeo |
| 101 | Simone Olman, Teebar Rodeo |
| 102 | Lisa Sutherland, Widgee Rodeo |
| 103 | Suzanne Brooks, Imbil Rodeo |
| 104 | Shea Fisher, Kenilworth Rodeo |
| 105 | Shandelle Armitage, Teebar Rodeo |
| 106 | Brooke Cavanagh, Kenilworth Rodeo |
| 107 | Jo Fisher, Widgee Rodeo |
| 108 | Janice Lancaster, Kenilworth Rodeo |
| 109 | Joanne Lawton, Kilkivan Rodeo |
| 110 | Jaime Cottam, Toogoolawah Rodeo |
| 111 | Tui Gordon, Teebar Rodeo |
| 112 | Kim Clarke, Kenilworth Rodeo |
| 113 | Kim Lange, Teebar Rodeo |
| 114 | Unknown, Laura Rodeo |
| 115 | Denae Hart and Troy Cavanagh, Teebar Rodeo |
| 116 | Scott Peters and Kerri Ann Young, Imbil Rodeo |
| 117 | Lisa Tynan, Widgee Rodeo |
| 118 | Rebecca Whitfield, Widgee Rodeo |
| 120 | Mick Hecksher, Caboolture Rodeo |
| 121 | Adam Purse, Laidley Rodeo |
| 122 | Steve Sutherland, Imbil Rodeo |
| 123 | Lex Bliesner, Gympie Rodeo |
| 124 | John Want, Widgee Rodeo |
| 125 | Alan Flood, Toogoolawah Rodeo |
| 126 | Scott Augustin, Teebar Rodeo |
| 127 | Brad Cavanagh, Widgee Rodeo |
| 128 | Mick Hecksher, Widgee Rodeo |
| 129 | Luke Gall, Teebar Rodeo |
| 130 | Marcus Jones and Dean Black, Kenilworth Rodeo |
| 131 | Michael Pearce and Jeff Harth, Widgee Rodeo |
| 132 | Neil Hesse and Jesse Townsend, Widgee Rodeo |
| 133 | Ken Pennell and Ben Bell, Widgee Rodeo |
| 134 | Matt and Lindsey Speedy, Widgee Rodeo |
| 135 | Scott Augustin, Gympie Rodeo |
| 136 | Scott Peters, Widgee Rodeo |
| 137 - 158 | Photos of the Juniors of the Sport. |